I0455691

# CHOICE

## Black America's Decision

A futuristic social essay that
transmits the seed of nation
formation for Black America

Brooks B. Robinson

## Dedication

Choice is dedicated to women in our lives who make choices to nurture and protect us—to at least ensure our survival. These women include our grandmothers (Clonzie and Sallie Mae); our mothers (Delia); our sisters (Vivian, Delia, and Angela); our wives (Wylma); and our daughters (Mariah and Michelle).

In honoring them, we remain true to certain African traditions in which lineage is passed down through females.

We only hope that this book will enable more Black women and men to make correct choices that will ensure the survival and preservation of Black Americans for the millennia                          ahead.

## Foreword

"Every day I have the blues..." The legendary B.B. King croons that tune from time-to-time on Black radio stations across America. Those words sum up, in part, the Black American experience. From the day a slave ship left the coast of West Africa transporting human chattel to the Western Hemisphere, Blacks have had the blues. What we know about the blues is that we can make them go away. How? We can turn to fried chicken, candied yams, collard greens, corn bread, apple cobbler, pound cake, or ice cream; a cigarette; a bottle of Thunderbird, Chianti, Jack Daniels, or Chivas Regal; a joint; a crack pipe; powder cocaine; a heroine needle; we can sing about it; we can make ourselves work-a-holics so that we don't have to think about it; or we can just hang out on the street corner and talk to other bloods about the blues. Alternatively, we can endure the pain of figuring out why Betsy or Susan got so upset that she left us in the lurch, commit ourselves to a seven-step process of atonement and reconciliation, and then go on with our lives. This tells us that, whatever we do about the blues, we make choices to make it go away, one way or the other.

From the very outset, we had the blues and we had choice ways of dealing with the blues. The present problem is that the entire world has the blues. There are global financial and economic crises. There is abject poverty on five of the world's seven continents. The current recession is producing hundreds of millions of unemployed workers. There are wars in Iraq and Afghanistan. Conflicts abound on the West Bank, in Sri Lanka, the Philippines, in the Stans, and elsewhere. There is racism, sexism, chauvinism, and income inequality everywhere we turn. But none of this is any worse than the blues, and the parties involved make choices everyday about how to address each issue.

On November 4, 2008, Barack Obama was elected President of the United States, and that event brought hope to Black Americans and to many people of the world. It marks the present era that is filled with hope and anticipation. But if we are wise, we will use our present circumstances as a time to make strategic decisions that will ensure our survival and that of our progeny.

The future stands before us as a time when our blues will still haunt us, when blues are a thing of the past, or when the blues have become the best friend of a people who have replaced us because we no longer exist. Essentially, we are at a turning point in the 21$^{st}$ century where our very future existence stands in the balance. Into the deep future, there will be people on the planet and elsewhere in the universe who have genes that are connected to those of today's Black Americans. However, if we are not careful, we may make choices that precipitate the very end of Black Americans as we know them today. Is this a choice that we want to make?

Because you are reading this futuristic social essay, you will not be able to say that you didn't know. You have a choice to think seriously about the circumstances that are highlighted in this book, to contemplate the affects of specific strategic actions, and then to make the correct choice. We hope that this book will motivate you to do just that. If it does not, then many will disappear from the planet not realizing that they could have been saved. But we all know that "my people or destroyed because of lack of knowledge." (*The Holy Bible*, Hosea, 4:6).

Please be forewarned that *Choice* will challenge your willingness to consider and accept new ideas and concepts. Certain aspects of the book may not sit well with you on first reading. However, after some thought and after a second or third reading, we hope that you will be able to reconcile yourself to the thoughts expressed herein.

*Choice* has three parts that walk us through the past, present, and future. The intent is to set us up for a realization of where we are in history, to emphasize the need to make good strategic decisions to preserve the history, culture, and life of Black Americans, and to guide Black America's future development.

Our contributions to the world have not yet been fully acknowledged. Our story will never be told if we fail to make the correct choices. For your sake, for the children's sake, and for the sake of the world, read *Choice* and make the correct choice!

# Table of Contents

# Part I: 1619 – 2008: Past

Few take the time to consider the counterfactual. What would the world have been like today if Africans had rejected entry by outsiders: Middle Easterners, Easterners, or Europeans? Early on, with their sense of grace and openness, they permitted outsiders to enter. Semites had come, the Greeks and Romans had come, the Arabs had come, and so it was not unexpected that Africans would welcome Europeans on the west coast. Those Europeans, however, initiated a period of history that has been nothing but the blues for those Africans who were brought to the Americas. Let's be clear: All along the way, people of African descent had choices.

Some exercised their choice by plotting overthrow, killing the crew, and returning to Africa (e.g., *La Amistad*). Some jumped overboard, preferring to be swallowed up by the great fish in the Atlantic Ocean than to be wrestled from their beloved homes, families, and tribes. Others prayed for death, refused to eat, and died in the holes of ships. Others, too young to comprehend the import of their journey sickened and died among the feces and vomit. Others, the strong and unyielding—maybe adventurous—did not give up or give in. They said within themselves, "I am a survivor, and I shall continue to exist for another day. I am going to hold on to God's unchanging hand, and I am going to wait until my change comes."

Not being historians, we cannot be expected to provide a full and accurate account of developments from the point of landing by African slaves on the shores of North America in 1619 in Virginia. Neither is that our purpose here. What we take note of is the beginning formation of a people who could become the saviors of the world. Remember that even Jesus had choices. Take a moment to recognize the connection between Jesus' birth from a virgin and the fact that Black Americans were inserted into virgin earth called Mary (A "Meri" ca) in a place called Virginia.

That fetus of a people experienced undue turmoil as they grew into shape. Yes, there was slavery in the north and in the south. Yes, Blacks have been known to say that there were "good" and "dastardly" masters. Imagine calling slave masters good. If they were good, it would be in the sense that they inherited slaves and could not, on their own accord, simply release slaves into a society that was unprepared to accept them and to nourish their development. On the other hand, there were many cases of free Blacks in the north and in the south who managed their survival. So we should check our assumptions about using the term "good" masters. There were none. On what grounds, and under what conditions, should one human being stifle the freedom of another human being? On the other hand, it is important to concede that there are righteous (and evil) persons among all races/ethnicities and religious groups. The *Holy Qur'an* (3:113-4) states this realization as follows:

> "Not all of them are alike: Of the people of the book are a portion that stand (for the right); they rehears the signs of God all night long, and they prostrate themselves in adoration. They believe in God and the last day; they enjoin what is right, and forbid what is wrong; and they

hasten (in emulation) in
(all) good works: They
are in the ranks of the
righteous. (The content
in parentheses reflects
the translator's
interpretation.)

Surmise it to say that Blacks found their
way through slavery. What choices did
they have? Some events unfolded in
response to circumstances. If you
happened to be appealing to the master,
you succumbed to his desires or paid a
high price. As a result of succumbing, you
likely produced offspring who were favored
by the master. You and your children
became "House Negroes." As such, you
experienced a warmer, tastier, cleaner,
more pleasant life than your counterpart
"Field Negroes." The latter endured the
lash, the heat, the pain, and the thirst. The
physical thirst, however, may not have been
more unquenchable than the thirst for
freedom. Blacks' choice has always been
freedom. Yet, Blacks have worked the
scenario with patience—"running with
patience the race that was set before them"
(*The Holy Bible, Hebrews* 12:1).

Black American patience wore thin from time-to-time. What were Denmark Vessey, Gabriel Prosser, and Nat Turner thinking? They were thinking freedom! Deep inside their psyche was an embedded—almost genetic—knowledge that the world is huge, and that men should be free to pursue happiness in any way that they choose. Man and woman were supposed to have choices. One of the most important of those choices was to be with the one that you loved.

It is common knowledge that in the African tradition, families engaged in arranged marriages, and so it was expected that some "other" would be selected for you. It turned out that you could learn to love the one chosen for you. On the other hand, you might also identify one who produced a burning in your loins, which created great desire. Who knows where you saw her; in the market, while traveling from one plantation to another, up in the big house, or down in the field. Wherever you saw her or him, your desire flamed. To be denied the opportunity to satisfy that longing was almost unbearable. Consider the days and nights of yearning in a society where you were denied. You had a choice: Run away together. You had a choice: Sneak around and grab fleeting moments of pleasure. You had a choice: Suffer in silence. You had a choice: Vow to kill the ones that blocked your access to the one that you loved most. Were Denmark, Gabriel, and Nat thinking along these lines? We have records recorded by those who analyzed the events of those famous insurrections, but do we have the full and undiluted truth. It's all about the blues. We might dress up our actions in swaddling clothes. However, often deep down, our actions are driven by the simple deep gut—deeper and lower than gut—desire to fulfill our yearnings.

So Blacks were in America. Separation by time and space made them forget about their fellow slaves in the Caribbean and in Central and South America. One day soon, all of Black America must return to the same page, pick up where they left off, and continue their development of the world as the original man and woman who know most and best how to make the world the place that God created. Don't forget that, when the European came, African languages didn't even include a word for "jail." Imagine that, no place to lock people up when they misbehaved. Obviously, you only need such places when you have created in your society conditions that

6

motivate anti-social behavior. Was it that African societies created no such conditions? Or if such behaviors surfaced, did Africans have more humane and intelligent ways of addressing the problem? Why jails? What mentality does that come from? Was it from a people whose short growing season and deadly winters caused them to be antisocial by nature in order to survive? Was it from a people who lived in dark, lonely, icy caves? Was it from a people who have little warmth, who respond to duty and survival, but not to love?

After a few generations, Black American slaves decided within themselves that slavery must be God's will and that there must be a purpose for the suffering. For a people who worshipped God in everything because God is everything and everywhere, Black Americans comprehended that nothing happens outside of God's will—and "according to his riches in glory" (*The Holy Bible, Philippians*, 4:19). Therefore, Black Americans knew that suffering could be redemptive and decided to endure the "suffering as a good soldier" (*The Holy Bible, 2$^{nd}$ Timothy*, 2:2). However, Black Americans decided to make the suffering as painless as possible.

Black Americans looked around and saw that there were ways to minimize the suffering. They learned how to please their masters. They became masters at bowing and grinning to please him. They understood that the quickest way to the heart of the coldest thief and liar is through his or her children. They made the master's children their children—even to the neglect of their own children. Black Americans eased the pain by becoming the loyal servants that they were expected to be. Much like religion, Black Americans worshiped their lord in the big house totally and completely so that they were not consumed by the hell on earth going on down in the quarters. What hell was going on down in the quarters? Well, John and Betsy were having a terrible time because John knows that the master is having sexual relations with Betsy and there isn't one thing that he can do about it.

Every day, John remembers the first time that he saw Betsy. She was the prettiest and sweetest thing that he ever saw. From that moment on, all he wanted was Betsy. He decided to be a good slave so that he might gain the opportunity to be with Betsy. The master agreed. However, the master soon came to realize what John had realized long ago; that Betsy was sweetest of the sweet, loveliest of the lovely, warmest of the warm, softest of the soft, and most flavorful of those who have flavor. The master's less sexually desirable wife was available, and he could endure her from time to time because he knew that heavenly Betsy was there for him when he called. She had to come because he had the authority and power to make it so.

Yes, John had the blues, and there wasn't a thing in the world that he could do about it. Well, that is not exactly true. Maybe he couldn't control the master's desires, but he could control his own response. Initially, he took it out on Betsy. Then he realized that she was in a "Catch 22." Not only that, John loved Betsy. He couldn't stand to see himself hurting her, so he began to withdraw. He could not talk about it. He could only think about it—every waking moment. Early in the morning as she poured his coffee and got dressed to go to the big house, he thought about her being around the master up there. When he dragged himself off to the field to hoe and chop cotton, he thought about Betsy and the master with every stroke of his hoe. When the sun reached its zenith at noon, he thought in his mind about how Betsy's warmth and fire was as hot as the sun and how that fire put him in ecstasy, yet she was with the master and not with him. In the evening, when the two of them returned to their shack in the quarters to eat supper and go to bed, he thought about all that she had done for the master and the misses all day, wondering whether the master had stolen her away for his own enjoyment, then took an afternoon nap. After supper, Betsy was tired and went to sleep. Although he too was exhausted, he could not go to sleep, he could only lie there thinking about the heaven lying next to him which he wanted to enter. And even when he did, she could not give herself fully to him because she was already used by the master. Every morning, every day, and every night this would go on. John had the blues.

John could have run away and risked being caught, whipped, or murdered. He chose none of those courses of action. Inherently, John was an economist, and he decided that "something was better than nothing." A little bit might suffice. He picked up his cross and followed. He went inward. He closed out the world. He endured. He thought more and talked less. He saw the world as hell and death as heaven. He became Christian-like. He survived. Then he died with his hopes unfulfilled and with his unrealized dreams turned into a nightmare. John lived and died with the blues.

It seems that much of slave America followed John's course. Slaves saw themselves as all alone in America, they were so distant from their African families, yet they loved each other too much to systematically make destructive efforts to wipe out slave owners and free themselves. Yes, they were outnumbered, but they should have known from their Qur'anic teachings that God can "visit you with angels" to assist in battle (*Holy Qur'an*, 3:124-125). On the other hand, maybe what we are missing here is wise African fables or tales that foretold of the Black American sojourn. In the Genesis it says, "and ye shall be strangers in a strange land for 400 years; after which, you will come out with great substance" (15:13-14). Maybe in their race consciousness they knew that if they endured, that their progeny would one day "come out with great substance."

What John did as he became older and wiser, when he talked less and thought more, was to "perfect the change." That is, he grasped the ability to release his internal winged soul from his body (the ka) in order to occupy the body of his son or daughter. He came to realize that the soul is truly eternal, that death had no power over him. He figured out that, at death, he could depart his physical body, and enter the body of his son or daughter and continue living. He figured that he could do this generation after generation until the day would come when the time was right to obtain the "great substance." Each generation would be a time to measure, plan, and fight a battle that involved "principalities and powers, and wickedness in high places" (*The Holy Bible, Ephesians*, 6:12). He understood that "the battle was not his, but the Lord's" (*The Holy Bible, 2^{nd} Chronicles*, 20:15). As a son of the Lord, he was due his inheritance, and if he endured patiently, he would receive his inheritance.

Somehow and somewhere from time-to-time prophets of God would appear to stir up the pot and move the process of redemption forward. Read the histories of Phyllis Wheatley, Harriet Tubman, Sojourner Truth, Olaudah Equiano, and Frederick Douglass and you will find that they made choices. They could have opted for a more conventional life. However, fate and the power of God propelled them forward to assume a journey that would move the Black American cause forward.

The Civil War was a case of God working not only in the south but in the north and outside of the Americas to produce a set of events that drove the nation to conflict. How did an Abraham Lincoln rise from such meager beginnings to play the role that he played in moving the nation to war and toward creating a set of different outcomes for Black slaves?

After the war, Black Americans took deliberative actions to improve their plight. They not only entered political arenas to remove old laws and to create new laws that were favorable for Black Americans, but they also moved aggressively to find their place economically in the American system. William Edward Burghardt (W.E.B.) Dubois shows in a seldom-cited study the fact that Black Americans saved more than Whites during the latter part of the 19th century and into the 20th century.[1] Those savings, according to Dubois, can be

---

[1] See "Negro Landholders of Georgia" in the *U.S. Bulletin of the Department of Labor*, No. 35.

assessed by the extent to which Blacks obtained title to land and other property all over the southeastern portion of the United States.

Moreover, Black Americans used the Freedmen's Bureau, their churches, and their social organizations to invest in one of the most important aspects of life—their education. They had already begun to do so in the north during the 1830's with the formation of the first historically Black College and Universities (HBCUs)—The Institute of Colored Youth. Normal schools formed everywhere and provided training for teachers who could go into Black communities all over the south to teach Black people the three R's. Blacks made a conscious choice to educate themselves. Before and after the Civil War, there are innumerable, untold stories about Blacks who taught themselves to read. We might go so far as to say that Black Americans' demand for publically sponsored education was the impetus for the current-day public education system in the United States.

Now that we are on education, let's pause to consider that important Booker T. versus W.E.B. controversy. In addition, let us consider Carter G. Woodson's critical set of essays on the *Mis-Education of the Negro*. First the former.   Actually, there was no controversy at all.  W.E.B. Du Bois simply stated a fact that is similar to the popularly recognized "20% - 80% Rule" today.  One aspect of the rule is that 20% of the population will earn or own 80% of the income.  Of course, during the 19$^{th}$ century, the rule was slightly different:   It was a "10% - 90% Rule."  In this case, 10% of the people would possess 90% of the formal education.   Consequently, DuBois was merely stating a logical fact; that there would be a talented 10$^{th}$ (see the *Souls of Black Folks*), which should play a special role in Black America.   Specifically, that 10% should be the *intelligencia* that could help direct Black America up the correct path toward development.  Although there seemed to be contention, the reality is that Booker     T.     Washington     simply acknowledged that the masses of Black Americans, the 90%, would not gain high levels of formal academic education, but would have to survive by the sweat of their brow.  He set out to ensure that as many Black Americans as possible be trained to perform their manual work functions well. We must recall that the level of technology available to Black Americans was very low at   that   time   (see   *Up   From   Slavery*).

Therefore, the so-called controversy was concocted. In our view there was general agreement, at least in theory, between Booker T. and W.E.B.

Probably a more important issue of the day was Carter G. Woodson's contention that the Negro was mis-educated. When you are made to believe that all aspects of the society in which you live were formulated by ancestors of the people in control of that society, and that your ancestors were savages with no intellects who contributed nothing to the past and, therefore, made no contributions to the present, then you must question your right to exist. What Dr. Woodson wanted Black Americans to know was that their ancestors had played a foundational role in the development of the world from the very outset.

What we learn from Dr. Woodson's 18 powerful chapters is that, from the earliest periods, Blacks in Africa played key roles in the development of modern economic, political, educational, and scientific systems. Given that Blacks are very religious people, as opposed to reading the Bible, they should have had the opportunity to read the *Egyptian Book of the Dead* (a.k.a., the *Book of Coming Forth by Day*) to learn details concerning their great origins. What they would have learned was that all of the key tenants of Judaism, Christianity, and, thereby, Muhammadanism (Islam) are found in the *Egyptian Book of the Dead*. Because Christianity formed the basis of European life, Blacks would have been clear that all that was European was first postulated in Africa. The critical link that needed to be made was that "Egyptian" meant African, meant Black. From the very outset, Europeans tried to convince Black Americans and Black people of the world that Egypt was "Middle Eastern," not Black Africa. Europeans tried their level best to delink Egypt from Africa, including Napoleon's famous effort to blow to smithereens the nose of the great Sphinx so that the facial likeness of the Sphinx with its broad nose and thick lips could not be linked to the Black people of Africa.

Now if you get down into the *Egyptian Book of the Dead* you will find that the Europeans will justify their attempt to separate Egypt from Africa using the famous references to the "dancing Pigmy" (see the Introduction to E. A. Wallis Budge's *The Egyptian Book of the Dead: The Papyrus of Ani).* The story is that a famous leader of Egypt requested that a Pigmy be brought to dance and entertain him. Of course, the Pygmy was brought from the interior of Africa; however, that fact does not destroy the link between Egypt and Africa—it only serves to strengthen it. To know about the Pygmy is to be familiar with one's surroundings and relatives who may have had unique characteristics due to slightly different genetics and climatic environments. Just because Pigmies are short and Egyptians may have been taller than Pigmies does not mean that they were not both Black people. The Maasai are taller than the Pigmy and they are Black; what precludes the Egyptians from being taller than the Pigmy and being Black. To attempt to delink Africa from Egyptians because the Egyptians were generally taller than the Pigmy is akin to delinking Nordic Europeans from the rest of Europe. Just because the Nordic people have whiter skin and blond hair does not make them less European than the slightly darker skinned and darker haired neighbors who live slightly further south on the European Continent.

What Dr. Woodson was attempting to get Black Americans to comprehend was that Africans were the primary source of life in the world as ultimately proven by Dr. David S. Leakey, and that Black Africans played a central role in the development of all types of knowledge: Economic, Political, Scientific, Mathematical, Chemical, Astronomical, Navigational, etc. If Black Americans had not been mis-educated (i.e., misinformed), then they would have had a different outlook on their role in the world and in America. Being separated from Africa by time and space, and with no way to communicate with their relatives and forefathers, they forgot their past and came to assume that they were nobodies— nothings in this vast world. They became rootless and treeless. This is the worst possible condition to experience in a world where every people justify their existence by their contributions. Feeling that they had contributed nothing made Black Americans feel that they were nothing. The reality is that Blacks founded it all, created it all, and own it all because they are the Great Father and Mother. "How can the son and daughter be greater than the Father and Mother who taught them?" Once Black Americans regain their connection to Africa, then they can reclaim their great place at the table of humanity. Black people of the world shall be recognized for their great contributions to the world and honored for it. Recognize that, just because something is hidden, does not mean that it does not exist.

When we arrive in the 20$^{th}$ century, like the rest of America, we find that Blacks endured the financial and economic crisis of 1907, and went on to fight in World War I (WWI). Black Americans leaped into the 1920s with vigor and underwent a great resurgence of self-identification and revelation during the Harlem Renaissance. We cannot underestimate the role of Marcus Garvey and the founding of the Universal Negro Improvement Association during the period. Marcus Garvey helped relink Black Americans to Africa and to the realization that Blacks had contributed much to the world and had every right to continue making great contributions to the world. The greatest expressions that could be made at that time were in the letters and in music. For the decade of the 1920s, Black America released a long blast of living air that carried with it enduring and endearing stories of Black life in America in the form of poetry, novels, essays, plays, and music. Black America told the world that they had been transplanted, had gone through living hell, but still had something to say about how life could and should be lived and expressed. Even the words "Harlem Renaissance" conjures up the idea of a great awakening that must have been fantastic to participate in and to live through. Throughout this period, Blacks continued to make contributions in the fields of science and engineering—making possible key developments in America's industrial development. (Think George Washington Carver and Granville T. Woods.)

The economic bust that was the 1930s represents the agony of the delivery of the Christ child (the baby Jesus), which was presaged by the great awakening and uncomfortableness of the 1920s. But to comprehend fully the birth of Jesus, we must make a slight detour through a conceptual development and a physical manifestation.

First, the conceptual development. We must always remember that things are not always as they seem. Remember that Blacks are in a war "not against flesh and blood, but against principalities and powers, and spiritual wickedness in high places" (*The Holy Bible, Ephesians* 6:12). Accordingly, men of righteousness must work shrewdly and wisely to effect change.

Sometimes that change may be subtle—sometimes the change is not so subtle. In the great battle of good versus evil, wise and righteous people gather periodically to advance the cause of man and his true relationship with God—the creator of it all, the "One." These wise and righteous people receive inspiration to gather and lay out a plan for man's development for the future. On the authority of Malcolm X (Malcolm Little, a.k.a. el-Hajj Malik el-Shabazz), who gained that authority from the Honorable Elijah Muhammad (a.k.a. Elijah Poole from Sandersville, Georgia), we are told that wise men met approximately 6000 years ago to write the future history of the world. That history was ultimately assembled in the religious books that we have before us today—*The Holy Bible* and the *Holy Qur'an*.[2]

It seems asinine to make this claim concerning books about which so much has been written concerning their origin. The

---

[2] It is important to note that scientist have recently confirmed the appearance of blue eyes between 6000 and 10,000 years ago; (see MSNBC, "Genetic Mutation Makes Those Brown Eyes Blue," March 21, 2008; http://www.msnbc.msn.com/id/22934464/wid/11915773).

reality is that mystery shrouds the origin of both books. In the case of the Old Testament, the supposed authors, the so-called Hebrew or Jewish people of the world cannot provide substantiating and unequivocal proof concerning the stories that constitute the Torah (Taurat) or many of the remaining writings. Councils have met over the course of history to assemble this book. If councils could meet to reconstruct and to write these books over the past 3000 years, why could a council not have met 6000 years ago to write the original work? It is also true that the life of the Jesus is also shrouded in mystery. To many, he is a mythical figure who appeared, lived, and then disappeared. It is very difficult to find evidence of this historical Jesus. It is instructive to learn today that great energy is being expended by scholars all over the world, but particularly by Jewish scholars, who seek to prove that the Jews were in Egypt— something that has not been proven beyond a shadow of a doubt.[3] We should

---

[3] In 2006, the History Channel broadcast a documentary, "Exodus Decoded," concerning the efforts by Jewish scholars to prove that Jews were in Egypt. Their most potent evidence was ancient paintings of a scene of travelers wearing colorful coats (Joseph's coat of many colors); one or a few

not forget that in the New Testament book of St. John 8:33, the Jews are said to tell Jesus, "We have never been in bondage to anyone" possibly meaning that they were not slaves in Egypt. In addition, recently, scholars have uncovered what they claim is a tomb that housed the bodies of Jesus and members of his family. These scholars use probability theory to justify the likelihood that they have found Jesus' burial place— the probability that one tomb would contain the combination of names associated with Jesus and his family members during the relevant historical period. Clearly, no one has been able to construct an air-tight case for developments in the Old and New Testament with clear evidence of all of the historical personages and of all of the events that are recorded. In other words, given the evidence that we have, it is equally plausible that much of the Bible could constitute a futuristic vision of things to come. (Can we here Nostradamus?)

---

ring insignia's that purportedly represented a "Joseph stamp," which was supposedly related to Joseph's rule of the store houses of Egypt and his authority to manage the economy; and inscriptions on a cave wall that are interpreted to mean "God, save us from these mines," which includes an ancient rendering of the Hebrew word for God (see http://en.wikipedia.org/wiki/Exodus_Decoded).

On the Qur'an, which is recognized as recitations from Prophet Muhammad ibn Abdullah (may the peace and blessings of Allah for ever be upon him), we are told that the revelations came from Gabriel. Gabriel is said to be an angel. What we know about religious literature and symbolism is that angels represent people (men or women) with power. They have wings, meaning that they have the knowledge to travel through time and space and to see and know that which ordinary persons cannot see and know. Why should we not surmise that one of the wise persons that were alluded to earlier was not Gabriel? Could it not be that a wise man dictated the Qur'an to the Prophet? Whether before or behind a veil, Prophet Muhammad received messages that were so consistent with the Old and New Testaments that it seems reasonable to believe that the same wise person or persons played a role in the construction of both religious texts.

That is the conceptual matter. For the physical manifestation, we must go back to the 19th century and to the birth of a Pakistani named Fard (فرد, alone, single, sole, unique, matchless) Muhammad. The literature on this personality says that he had many names during his sojourn in

America. What escapes us is the precise points of his arrival and departure from the United States. Like God's unknowability, we may never know all that there is to know about Fard Muhammad. What we will learn from this futuristic social essay is that in most respects, he is the creator of a new man, woman, and child in North America—a people who were raised up, brought into existence, by Jesus (the Honorable Elijah Muhammad), and who will form a new nation that will survive and reign over the world. Like God, the people that he formed will never have seen him, yet they will believe in him. His son (the Jesus), the one to whom he imparted knowledge and guided like a good father is inclined to do, was the Honorable Elijah Muhammad. We must remember that even in the New Testament, when the Jews are attempting to determine who Jesus was, Jesus said to them, "and who say you that I am. And they replied some say that you are Elijah."[4] What we know today, is that the wise writers of old knew that the Jesus to come

---

[4] There are numerous references to "Elijah" in the Synoptic Gospels, mainly concerning efforts to identify Jesus as a return of an important Hebrew Prophet. See for example, St. Mark 6:15; St. Matthew 17:3; and St. Luke 1:17.

would be known as Elijah. What we can say about Fard Muhammad, the God of Black America, is that "he so loved the world that he gave his only begotten son, so that whomsoever believeth on him shall not perish, but will have everlasting life" (*The Holy Bible, John* 3:16).

Fard Muhammad so loved the world in the sense that he gave his son the religion of peace (Islam) a religion that was not a violent religion that would have called for the murder of the White world for its dastardly deeds against the Black world. God gave his only begotten son. Elijah Poole was not God's (Fard Muhammad's) actual or blood son, but he begot him by imparting to him the principles of Islam and the resurrection. Fard Muhammad could have taken his son with him when he departed America, but he left him in America and left him open to the vagaries of life in America—a life that was threatened many times, but a life that could not be destroyed. Yes, they crucified Jesus (the Honorable Elijah Muhammad), but they did not kill him (see the Holy Qur'an 4:157). He lived on to make true the revelation that "whomsoever believes in him shall not perish, but shall have ever lasting life" (*The Holy Bible, John* 3:16).

Actually, Elijah Muhammad was born on October 7, 1897, but it was in the 1930s that he promulgated the Nation of Islam and began his work as the Jesus—the one who would "save his people from their sins" (*The Holy Bible, Matthew 1:21*). Later we will see how he is expected to ensure that those who believe in him shall not perish and how they will have access to everlasting life. Now we simply recount how he saved his people from their sins.

The teachings of the Honorable Elijah Muhammad were sufficient to place Black America on a solid historical and scientific footing. Black America was in sin. Black America had adopted lifestyle behaviors that were destroying them—behaviors that were against the laws of nature. Much of Black America was "not fit for anybody"—themselves or the world. The teachings of the Honorable Elijah Muhammad were sufficient to transform and renew alcoholics, drug addicts, wife beaters, child molesters, gamblers, thieves, murderers, adulterers, fornicators, and any other type of sinner known to man. By transforming the lives of these lost souls, the Honorable Elijah Muhammad (Jesus) brought Black Americans into the natural order of things and filled hearts and minds with the old knowledge that is African. He rescued Black Americans and turned their hearts and minds back to their fathers in the east—Africa.

What is the essential knowledge of Africa? It is that man/woman can live forever. How does man live forever? This is achieved through a very special process of directing the souls of dying fathers and mothers into the bodies of their sons and daughters. The Black man and woman had forgotten this African—Egyptian knowledge. Jesus (Elijah Muhammad) brought this knowledge back to the hearts and mind of Black America. Given this knowledge, the entire world changes. How and why? Because even if one cannot achieve one's goals and aspirations during this life, it does not mean that one should not initiate or continue the work, it just means that one must be certain to remain clean and pure (Muslim like) so that one can effect the appropriate "change" at the conclusion of life—transporting the soul from the dying body to the living body of a like-minded son or daughter. Under such arrangements, one has no desire for war or destruction, just for the continued building up and advancement of mankind. Under such conditions, man and woman want the world to advance and to not be destroyed. Why should one hate, when life is eternal and there is plenty of time to solve problems and differences that may crop up. It was a reawakening of the African mind and spirit in the hearts and mind of Black America. This is what Jesus (Elijah Muhammad) brought. He was the savior for Black America. He saved Black America from her sins and brought the chance for everlasting life.

You say, "but wasn't Malcolm really Black America's shining prince—the "Prince of Peace? Was not Malcolm X really the Jesus?" No. Malcolm X was an extension of Jesus, just as Minister Louis Farrakhan is an extension of Jesus. "But Malcolm X was killed by the Muslims just as Jesus was killed by the Jews," you say. Wrong! Jesus was never killed—neither the historical Jesus, nor the manifestation of Jesus in the form of the Honorable Elijah Muhammad.

You ask, "If the Honorable Elijah Muhammad was Jesus, then he must have been born of a virgin named Mary." Well, it is instructive that the continents called "America" include the word "Meri" which is equivalent to Mary. It is true that America represents a virgin land. In addition, as referenced earlier, African slaves entered North America through Virginia. It is also true, that in the context of America, the "man" in America was the White man. The Honorable Elijah was birthed with a divine mind in order to become the Jesus without the agency of a White man (a man) in Mary (America). This is the mystery of the virgin birth. It is important to add that this Jesus of a man, the Honorable Elijah Muhammad, was visited by wise men from the east, who came to honor him and his Black American people.

If the Honorable Elijah Muhammad is the real Jesus for Black America, then Black Americans must be the real Jews. Correct! Black Americans are those who were and are "strangers in a strange land for 400 years, after which they will come out with great substance" (*The Holy Bible, Genesis* 15:13-14). Yes, the real Jews are God's chosen people. They are a people who have been molded into shape in a fiery furnace of slavery affliction, racism, discrimination, poverty, and ignorance. However, after that shaping of 400 years, God has produced a people that are truly empathetic to the needs of the world and who know how to meet the needs of the world. They were without love, so they yearn for and know how to give love. They were without care, so they know how to give care. They were without nurture, so they learned how to nurture. They were without the gifts of the spirit so they meditated on and learned how to exercise the gifts of the spirit, which are: "Love, Joy, Peace, Patience, Kindness, Goodness, Faithfulness, Gentleness, Self-Control, against such there is no law" (*The Holy Bible, Galatians* 5:22-23). The evidence was before us all along. Blacks used to, and still, sing in their churches today, "When God gets through with me, I shall come forth as pure gold." If gold is of the highest value, then what is more valuable to the sustainability of human life than the qualities just described?

The Honorable Elijah Muhammad (Jesus) said that the White world would never accept Black America. He said, "You will never be accepted by the White man." He said that Black Americans should establish their own land, their own nation, their own country. Do you agree? Why will the White world never fully accept the Black man? Think about it! If you had raped, robbed, stolen, emasculated, bludgeoned, murdered, lied on, and defiled another man, would you ever expect him to forgive you—

even if you had tried to convince him that he needed to forgive you in order to enter heaven after he died. The White man could never trust you to forgive him. He could never afford to trust you in his most inner circle. If you entered his inner circle, there would always be the threat that you would turn on him and destroy him. Because no man wants to be destroyed, it is against the very law of nature for him to trust someone who is apt to destroy him. Therefore, the White world will never accept members of the Black world—unless members of the Black world are so well trained that they show, beyond a shadow of a doubt, that they can be trusted to not destroy the evil force that sought to destroy them.

To make life livable, somewhat beyond a point of eternal fear that Blacks would turn on Whites, Whites spend an inordinate amount of effort teaching Christianity to Blacks. It is a religion that features a White Jesus who is said to be the son of God. As the great Black American historian John Henrik Clarke points out in his famous lecture, "The African Mind" (hear this lecture at http://odeo.com/episodes/3942293-John-Henrik-Clarke-The-African-Mind), that Black Americans will kill each other if one steps on the other's freshly shined shoes, but they will not lay a hand on a hair of a member of the White world—even if Whites do all manner of evil against them—because the Black world views Whites in the image of Jesus—the son of God. In other words, Blacks do not want to jeopardize their chances of reaching heaven. Now the truth has come and the world has changed. The truth is that heaven is the world that we make for ourselves on earth—a place where we live everlastingly as we change the soul from our dying body into the living body of our children. Given our hope of eternal life, we work to make this life—especially the lives of our children—as pleasant as possible because it is in their bodies that we shall live on forever and ever. This is the way of our fathers, the way of our ancestors. Those who know this truth shall be set free. Free from what. Free from the ignorance of death, free from the ignorance of what to do upon death, free from the mystery of death. What is life all about? It is about living forever in the bodies of our children, grandchildren, and great grandchildren. Life is about building for the next generation, because it is in that generation that we shall live. Don't be distracted, come into the knowing.

Despite this guidance from Jesus ("they shall never accept you"), Black Americans opted to fight in the U.S. courts for desegregation and integration during the 1950s and 1960s. These Blacks were bamboozled! They were sold a faulty concept and a faulty product. They concluded that the wealth and lifestyle of the White world was more appealing than life in the Black World. Please do not be confused. We are not saying that equality is inappropriate. We agree that every man and woman should have equal rights under the law. Remember the Honorable Elijah Muhammad (Jesus) taught, "What do we demand? We demand: Freedom, Justice, and Equality." Yes, it was and is appropriate to fight for Freedom, for Justice, and for Equality. However, Black Americans should have in no way fought for desegregation or integration.

It is possible to prove, in a limit of time, that Black America would have been better off today than it currently is, if Black America had fought just for Freedom, Justice, and Equality. That would have entailed expenditures of funds in Black America to raise the standard of living and to enforce laws that would have produced justice and equality. Whether one considers the economic, political, educational, health, or any other conditions of Black America, one will find that the loss of the talented 10$^{th}$ to the suburbs as a result of integration has left Black America worse off overall. If Black America had opted for separate and self-development, all of Black America would have been better off. The number and quality of Black business, the number of political representatives, the quantity and quality of education, Black health, and every other aspect of Black America would have been better off, if Black leadership had not escaped to the suburbs.

Recall that in the 17$^{th}$, 18$^{th}$, and 19$^{th}$ centuries, Black Americans sought to escape slavery by leaving the plantation. White America turned the table upside down in the 20$^{th}$ century and caused Black America to invert their escape actions. From the 1960s to the turn of the 21$^{st}$ century and beyond, Black America began to escape to slavery in the suburbs. How is living in the suburbs slavery? Because a Black man or woman who lives in the suburbs must willingly place handcuffs on their wrists, but more importantly, on their minds to prevent him or her from taking the action that a normal human being would take. You must completely and totally submit your soul to a White Christ, and ignore your normal conscious and nature that tells you to kill the White man and woman who performed so many dastardly deeds against you and your ancestors that they cannot be numbered. Yet Black Americans have been so conditioned by their experience in America that they enter voluntary servitude to be a slightly fatter rat in a rat maze than their Black American counterparts in the ghetto.

How do Black Americans get freedom, justice, and equality? They can ensure their own freedom, justice, and equality, by founding their own Black nation. Where should this nation be founded? The Jesus, the Honorable Elijah Muhammad, said that it should be in America. Within the past 20 years, Black Americans have performed a mass reverse migration back to the southern United States. Some may argue that Jesus called for the establishment of a Black nation in the southern United States. But it may be worthwhile to consider the religious text and to enquire about what it says. The answer is that the land to be granted was called Canaan. In North America, there is a land called Canada. If one removes a "d" from "Canada" and adds an "n," then one arrives at the word "Canaan," which could mark "d" "n" (the end) of the Black sojourn in America. Is there additional rationale for considering Canada (Canaan) as the site of the Black American nation? In the context of global warming and climate change, scientists predict that areas near the equator are likely to become warmer—unbearably so—while higher latitudes will also experience warmer temperatures. In other words, in the course of time, Canada may become a favorable environment for establishing the Black nation. Black America should be cautious in this endeavor and avoid creating conflict with the Native American people. Black America would be well advised to inquire of their Asiatic brothers for a part of the great land of America known as Canada to become their Canaan—the land that was promised to Black America by God as recorded in the Taurat and the teachings of the Honorable Elijah Muhammad.

The Lord Jesus of Black America has come! The truth is here! What do we do now? We live in precarious and perilous times. The 6000 year rule of the White man has ended. His world is nearly dead and bankrupt. Yet it gasps for life. The western world, especially the United States, has become the great parasite which is sucking the world dry of capital and brains. While the Asian, African, and South American continents seek to grow and develop, the Western world stifles that development by attracting the best and brightest minds from around the world. Moreover, western markets are manipulated to appear to be more safe and secure and with greater prospects for future growth such that capital that could accrue higher returns in emerging market and developing countries is being absorbed into the dying economies of Europe and the United States. Randall Robinson wrote "Quitting America" in 2005. He may be offering good advice to Black America. Now may be the appropriate time for Black Americans to Exodus and initiate their new nation in Canaan. Remember that the Jews exited Egypt across the Red Sea. The Red Sea today is that sea of red ink that characterizes the United States' fiscal condition—and it shall for the foreseeable future. Now is the appointed time for Black Americans to depart America and move into Canaan.

Is the Old and New Testament being confused here? We started with Jesus being the Honorable Elijah Muhammad, now the reference is to Jews exodusing into Canaan. We must remember that the New Testament states that "Jesus came not to destroy the law, but that through him the law might be fulfilled" (*The Holy Bible, Matthew* 5:17). What was the law? The law was not the "10 Commandments," per se. The law was the covenant that God made with his people. What did that covenant entail? It entailed the promise of Canaan (*The Holy Bible, Deuteronomy* 1:8). The Honorable Elijah Muhammad came to fulfill that covenant, by saving his people from their sins and by preparing them to enter Canaan.

Unfortunately, at a point when Black Americans should be preparing to enter Canaan, they are swooning over a contrived political event that placed a man who is part African and part White (a Semite) American in the White House. How did Barack Obama rise so fast? Who were his supporters? Why did the press treat him with "kid gloves" and mainly respond favorably to him? Why were equally qualified Black candidates treated so differently by the press and by the American public before the advent of Barack Obama? Does Barack Obama portend the great substance spoken of in the covenant—"after which they will come out with great substance?"

At a critical point when Jesus came to save his people from their sins, Black Americans opted for desegregation and ultimately integration. Wrong Choice. In 2008, when Black Americans should be moving to realize the fulfillment of the covenant by claiming Canaan, they opt to continue their enamoration with the golden calf—while still in the Wilderness of North America. Wrong Choice. The Red Sea is before Black America. When will you cross? Will you cross? Or will you forfeit your blessing in favor of worshipping the golden calf? Let us examine these queries as we consider "The Present" in Chapter Two.

## Appendices to Part I: 1619 – 2008: Past

Part I contains ideas and concepts that may be unfamiliar to readers, or they may be orthogonal to most readers' idea set. Consequently, we provide the following three Appendices to attempt to reorient readers' thinking somewhat.

## Appendix A: Transmission of the soul

In Part I, we promulgate the idea of inserting the living soul from a dying body into the living body of an offspring. This may be characterized as a type of Hindu or Buddhist concept or belief. Hindus and Buddhists believe in reincarnation—but mainly from an intertemporal perspective. That is, they believe that when a human body dies, the living soul leaves the body and then transitions through various stations before entering the womb of an expectant mother to be reborn with the child that occupies the mother's womb. Tibetan Buddhist believe that Dalai Lamas are enlightened and elevated enough to foresee their reincarnation. Dalai Lamas forecast where they expect to be reborn, and they provide hints concerning the child in which they are to be reborn. Therefore, the idea of near-term or immediate reincarnation has a good basis in principle, and may be believable to billions of Hindus and Buddhists in the world—although in a slightly different configuration. Whereas they believe that there is a gap in time from the point of death to reincarnation, we espouse here the idea that the soul can have an immediate transmission from one body to the next.

Appendix B: On Fard Muhammad as God and Elijah Muhammad as Jesus

In order to reconcile one's self to our characterization of Fard Muhammad as God and the Honorable Elijah Muhammad as Jesus, one must recognize that accepting new ideas or concepts is all about context. When we are born, we know nothing of formal religion. We are indoctrinated into a formal religion through our family and culture. We come to believe much of what we believe because we are invited or coerced into doing so. Suppose others have gotten it wrong. Suppose that the religious teachings that have been passed down have been misconfigured? Just because millions of people believe a concept, doesn't mean that the concept is true. Remember that, before Columbus "discovered" America, most of the people of Europe believed that the world was flat. Therefore, we believe that we are justified in calling for a new interpretation of the Bible and of history. The validity of our claims will be proven in the course of time.

One point to keep in mind is that Jesus Christ of Nazareth's story was one of a Jew who brought a new teaching—one that differed markedly from the widely-held teachings of the day that were taught by the Pharisees and the Sadducees. Similarly, the Honorable Elijah Muhammad was a Black American who brought a new teaching, which was quite different from that which was being taught in the Christian Church by Black religious scholars. Notably, the Honorable Elijah Muhammad, although he was known as a Black Muslim, taught more from the *Holy Bible* than he did from the Muslim's book, the *Holy Qur'an*. In our view, the Honorable Elijah Muhammad's story, the context, and the results of his efforts parallel those of Jesus.

Likewise, the story of Black Americans parallels the story of Jesus.

As we think about misinterpretations of important religious principles, we are reminded of a story that was going around on the Internet some while back. We found the story, as told by Lalit Mohan, on the Internet at the following Web site: http://www.indianexpress.com/news/the-art-of-copying/314344/.

> A young monk arrives at a monastery and is asked to help other monks in copying old canons and laws of the church by hand. He notices, however, that all of them are copying from copies, not from the original manuscript. So, he tells the head abbot that if someone made even a small error in the first copy, or dropped a word or a letter, it would be repeated in all the subsequent copies.

The head monk gets the point. He goes down into the dark cave underneath the monastery where the original manuscripts are held in a vault that has not been opened for centuries. Hours go by and nobody sees him. The younger man gets worried and goes down to look for him. He sees him, poring over originals, banging his head against the wall and wailing, "Somewhere, we dropped the R. The word was CELEBRATE."

Believe it or not, simple errors can lead us far astray from the truth and for extended periods of time.

Appendix C: Why the focus on Islam?

Our focus on Islam needs to be explained. It is a well known fact that a high percentage of the Africans who were brought to the Americas from West Africa were Muslims. Islam is a religion with which we were very familiar before coming to America. Moreover, we should be clear about what Islam is: Islam is simply submission to the will of God. If God is almighty and we want to worship God, then we should all be willing to submit to the will of God—i.e., be a Muslim. Now whether we believe that it is important to follow the tenants of religion set forth by Prophet Muhammad is another matter. In this case, we are abstracting from the latter point, and focusing on the work of the Honorable Elijah Muhammad who identified himself as a Black Muslim, but who, as we denote in Appendix B, taught mainly from *The Holy Bible*.

We are warranted in highlighting the fact that *Choice* is not about the use of the identifiers Hinduism, Buddhism, Judaism, Christianity, or Islam. No, it is about using our intellects to achieve outcomes that are favorable for life and doing so by using all of the information and knowledge that are at our disposal.

# Part II:  2008 – 2012:  Present

On November 4, 2008, Black, White, Hispanic, Asian, Native, and other Americans went to the polls and elected Barack Obama as the 44th president of the United States by a sizeable majority.  How significant was that event?  It will take some time to tell.  However, several results are quite transparent.  One fact about which there can be little disagreement is that the power of the media was apparent in the entire Obama entry on to the scene and his ascendancy to the presidency.  Given his very limited political experience and lack of exposure to the nation, it was anomalous that he would be given an opportunity to serve as a keynote speaker during the 2004 Democratic National Convention.  No question about it, some persons had a plan, and part of that plan was to place the face of a Black person in the Oval Office.  We cannot deny that the planners chose well.  Obama has great intellectual and physical appeal.  Notably, he had no long-standing political or legislative record about which to speak.  It did not hurt that he and his wife, Michelle, had packaged an almost ideal family image.  In any event, the rise from the 2004 speech at the Democratic National Convent was nearly automatic—a foregone conclusion. As early as the spring of 2007, it was apparent to us that he would be president, and we said as much in a short video essay (http://www.blackeconomics.org/Quickstart/VideoLib/BOOC.wmv).

Several related outcomes are quite disheartening from a Black American perspective. First, it was abnormal for the press and all of America to welcome the advent of Obama, given that they treated previous Black American presidential candidates so harshly. Think of Congresswoman's Shirley Chisholm's run, Jessie Jackson's two attempts, and Al Sharpton's efforts. Congresswoman Chisholm was brilliant. Jessie Jackson was knowledgeable. Yet neither fit the cookie-cutter framework that the press and America were looking for at the time. Obama was trained in the correct schools, had the Semitic look, and otherwise met the requirements of the planners who wanted to place a Black face in the White House.

Why was an Obama necessary? An Obama was required because America was losing face all around the world. Her credibility was in jeopardy. No matter how successful the media had been in the past in creating a positive image of America, the positive effect was wearing thin due to the poor decision-making of the 2000–2008 Bush Administration. The wars in Iraq and Afghanistan, because they constituted a comedy of military and public relations errors, did not help the situation. It was time for a Kennedyesk figure to come along to regenerate in the world a "love America" mentality and an era of good feeling. The media followed the 2008 presidential campaign around the nation and around the world all the way up to the election, and seemed to find that there was genuine love for Barack Obama. That love began to generate a rise in positive sentiments for the United States: From the Jakarta school that Obama attended as a child, to Obama City in Japan, to Kenyan villages where the Obama clan originated, there was a positive outpouring of care and respect for him. The press covered these expressions and created a hype that snowballed Obama all the way into the White House.

The most disheartening aspect of the entire process was the fact that Black Americans jumped on the Obama bandwagon. Black Americans forgot that, "if it looks too good to be true, then it probably is." Moreover, our studies show that popular Black American candidates do not generally improve outcomes for Black Americans where it counts—in their pocket book (see http://www.BlackEconomics.org/BE&Future/WWOPM.pdf). We must ask, "Why would Black Americans throw their full support behind a candidate who was not a "Black American"—a descendant of Black slaves? Were Black Americans so desperate for recognition and for acceptance that they were willing to turn head-over-heels for a figure that was manufactured by those sitting at the highest points of power in America to perform a task that had little relation to producing improved outcomes for Black Americans? At a point when Black Americans should be moving toward establishing their own nation, why would they fall into lock-step with a nation that is steadily meeting its demise in the world? Why go with a loser? As Malcolm X once said, "only a Negro" would turn a blind eye to his own blessing and opportunity in order to assist his White master!

Now, it is all water under the bridge. Obama is in office. What did it achieve for Black America? What will it bring? For Black Americans who have benefited most from integration (both the individuals and organizations such as the National Association for the Advancement of Colored People and the Urban League—both "front-line" organizations), it meant having somewhat increased access to the U.S. Treasury. While Obama probably has somewhat less power than preceding presidents, we recognize that no president has that much power. Not only does the organizational design of the United States prevent a concentration of power (executive, legislative, and judicial branches), but those who are familiar with the role of special interest in the "iron triangle" know that business drives outcomes in Washington. Owners of large and powerful firms ultimately get what they want—whether a particular president or congressperson wants it or not.

If one were to go back and read press pieces in key newspapers such as *The New York Times* and the *Washington Post* leading up to and shortly after the 2009 inauguration, one would find that there were a plethora of stories about the rising significance of previously little known Black personalities. All of a sudden, it became fashionable to have a Black face at the dinner party tables or in the drawing rooms of the real decision makers—White businessmen. The rich get richer. How? The rich remain rich and expand their wealth by being wise about how to "snow" the public and to maintain favorable sentiments within the populace. Obama's leadership of the United States, we must remember, follows Kofi Anan's leadership of the United Nations. Kofi Anan was akin to a puppet as is President Obama. To some extent, all presidents are puppets. Remember the words from Obama's mouth: He was not to be a Black, Asian, or Hispanic president, but an American president. Who owns America? Black Americans do not own America. For whom would Barack Obama work? He must work for the owners of America who are mainly White males.

It is important to recognize that Black America followed Obama and supported him mainly because high profile Blacks followed and supported him. Why did this occur? High-profile Blacks stood to benefit from an Obama presidency either because their own opportunities for increased wealth were likely to be enhanced, or because they were coerced into supporting Obama by their bosses.

What Black America needs to be aware of is that income inequality in America is greatest among Black Americans. That is, rich and powerful Blacks (the top 10 or 20 percent, you choose your measure) own a higher percentage of the income and wealth in the Black community than do the rich in the Asian, Hispanic, or White communities. We can use a statistical convention, *Gini* ratios, to assess income inequality across ethnic communities in the United States. *Gini* ratios can assume values between 0 and 1. A *Gini* ratio of 0 indicates perfect equality (i.e., every household has identical income), while a *Gini* ratio of 1 indicates perfect inequality (i.e., one household has all of the income). The lower the *Gini* ratio, the better—that is, the greater the equality. If we consider data from 2007, we find that the *Gini* ratio for the nation was .443; the *Gini* ratio for White households was .433; and the *Gini* ratio for Black households was .472. Income inequality is greatest among Black Americans—being 0.039 *Gini* points higher than income inequality among Whites, and 0.029 *Gini* points higher than income inequality for the nation. (The *Gini* ratio was .414 for Asians and .432 for Hispanics.) The differences between the Black, White, and the national *Gini* ratios are different in a statistically significant sense, meaning that the gaps conveyed by the *Gini* ratios are "real."[5]

Wealthy Blacks, many of whom are the "House Negroes" of the 21$^{st}$ century, supported Obama out of self interest or out of some misinformed belief that he would be good for Black America. Maybe they wanted to avenge their emasculation by Whites; maybe they thought that electing a Black President would be some sort of revenge. What they failed to recognize was that Obama had been hand-picked to be president, and that he would become president with or without them. In any event, most wealthy Blacks got on the bandwagon that carried Obama up to 1600 Pennsylvania Avenue.

Many not-so-wealthy Blacks did not necessarily support Obama, they supported Michelle Robinson—Obama's wife. It would be interesting to study how many Black women voted for Obama simply because of Michelle. What we know is that, all across the nation, many a Black

---

[5] These data can be found in the "Annual Social and Economic Supplement" to the *Current Population Survey* (http://pubdb3.census.gov/macro/032008/hhinc/new02 000.htm).

woman, especially those with a college-level education, joined and worked in the Obama campaign. A key determinant of their support was the fact that they respected Michelle. She is a regal figure that is true to the African tradition. Part of what Black women saw in Michelle was a Black woman who had a successful "Black" husband—something that is becoming increasingly rare.

Everyone knows the statistics: 49% of prisoners in the United States are Black males, while Black Americans constitute less than 14% of the U.S. population. How can this be? Increasingly, studies are showing that Black Americans end up in prison due to wrongful incarceration. A recent book, the authors and story of which were featured on an early 2009 *60 Minutes* episode, *Picking Cotton*, is typical of the faulty nature of the American criminal justice system. Moreover, it is common knowledge that Black males experience the highest exoneration rates when it comes to appeals of rape cases.

What we know from Jerry Kang's masterful March 2005 *Harvard Law Review* article, "Trojan Horses of Race," is that a Black man as criminal is deeply ingrained in the psyche of America. The media has been so effective at transmitting this message that it is virtually automatic in the thinking of most of America and around the world. Now the media is moving forward with a new story line. Not only are Black males criminals, but they are homosexuals and they have contracted AIDS in prison. Therefore, do not touch them. If you do, you are subject to contract AIDS and die.

But none of this should be unexpected, the *Holy Qur'an* (2:49) makes it clear that, in the land of Pharaoh, they will "slaughter your sons and let your women folk live." It is beyond the scope of this book to delve into why the European mind wants to destroy the Black male and retain the Black female. Suffice it to say that as we travel around the world physically or virtually via the media, we find increasing efforts to transform the masculine into the feminine. A male has a particular temperament. He thinks in a particular way. He can be aggressive; i.e., he can be a warrior. If your goal is to dominate the world, you would be best positioned to do so if you transform prospective opposition into a state where aggressive resistance to your objective is not forthcoming. You can accomplish this by making those most likely to oppose your plan, as Richard Prior used to say, "null and void." Make them sissies, and they will not fight you. From long hair, to tight fitting clothes, to sweet smelling colognes, males around the world are being transformed into beings who see themselves as "beautiful" or "pretty" more so than as men whose job it is to protect and defend their societies from the onslaught of a European mind that wants to maintain control of the entire world.

Black women are facing this issue head on. More and more Black men look more and more like Black women. Too many are homosexuals. Too many have contracted AIDS. What is the Black woman to do for a partner? If the goal of life is to produce children in which one can insert one's soul at the point of death to gain eternal life, how can one produce such children in a wholesome and healthy environment if the male is in jail or a homosexual? If he has AIDS, then you risk your own life in the procreation process. What's a Sister to do?

Several options are being proposed for the Black female. First, she can give up on having children and, thereby, create a desired outcome from a European perspective—reduced Black population growth. The argument is that, without children, Black women can have a "higher quality of life" because resources will not have to be directed toward caring for children. Second, to fulfill the inherent need for sexual relations, she can turn to another Black female or associate with a female of another ethnicity. A third choice, and one that is becoming increasingly popular, is for Black women to marry White males. A fourth choice, which has always been an option is for "good" Black men to engage in informal polygamous relationships. How would Black Americans respond to a Prophet Muhammad-like decision to authorize polygamy when the ratio of females to males is out of kilter?

What Black females must remember is that they are the mothers of civilization. Consequently, Black males are the fathers of civilization. For the world to be correct, mothers and fathers must join in holy matrimony and produce holy children to populate the world. In the great drama that constitutes the history of the world, the last 6000 years have featured an effort by a strange and evil mind to gain control of, and rule, the world. When we observe such good versus evil dramas in today's media, it is usually a foregone conclusion that good will triumph over evil. Actually, such an outcome is not guaranteed. As in the media, superhuman efforts may be required for good to overcome evil. Who can produce such superhuman efforts? Who built the pyramids? The Black man and woman as part of their holy society built the pyramids and ruled the known world even before the European crawled around in the caves of Europe. In order to restore sanity and peace to the world, including a world where humans can enjoy eternal life, the basic building block of society must be reconstituted. The world must reproduce the Black family of old, a family with a Black man and woman as the head, and with holy children who can serve as the vessels that carry life and civilization forward.

Black women should do all that they can to support good Black men in their efforts to reconstitute the holy Black family. Black men must do all that they can to regain the knowledge that is required to build and sustain the holy Black family. Together, male and female, man and woman, father and mother, can make all of this a reality. It begins with a decision to "do the right thing." The knowledge is embodied in the teachings of the Honorable Elijah Muhammad—the Black man's Jesus.

Another key step for Black men is to reject media efforts to transform maleness into femaleness. Cut the long hair, put off clothes that are designed to make the male body appear as a female body, discard the diamond earrings, and discontinue purchasing expensive colognes that make males smell sweeter than females. If the truth be known, a sweet smelling male reduces the female's appetite for the male, while a sweet smelling female increases the male's appetite for the female. If chemistry is important, and we know that sexual desire is highly stimulated through olfactory receptors, then let us get the chemistry correct in order to optimize correct relationships and to produce more and more Black children to populate the new Black nation that is being formed as we speak.

When the Biblical Jews were in the wilderness en route to Canaan, they began to grumble about having left the warm confines of their master's house in Egypt. They said, "Moses why have you brought us all the way out here to die, we had it good back in Egypt" (*The Holy Bible, Exodus* 10:10-12). Black Americans may be even more obstinate about moving forward to their new nation. Even before they depart for the transition to their new nation, they may balk at the idea, saying "Look how comfortable our lives are in the United States of America. We have apartments, and houses, and cars. We have a little change in the bank. We have doctoral degrees. We travel around the world from time-to-time, when our White bosses send us on an errand." What they forget is that they are not in control of their lives. This brings us to noted economist Joan Robinson's conclusion. Specifically, Robinson deduced that the Bushmen of South Africa experienced a higher quality of life than a professional worker in a Western society. Why? Because while the Western society professional had but one choice when he or she awakened each morning—that of "go to work"—the Bushmen had numerous choices: Till a garden, hunt in the nearby forest, fish in the local stream, walk to the nearest community for a visit with a friend, or do absolutely nothing. One must ask, "What is the benefit of a modern technological society if the most highly valued and demanded action is to perform essentially meaningless work?"

While it is true that Black women have closed the gap, and in many cases exceed the previous gap, between their wages and those of white women, it is also true that Black males and females have not closed the gap between their wages and the wages of White males. Studies show that Black males and females pay relatively more for high valued commodities, such as homes and cars (see John Yinger's 1995 article in the *American Economic Review*, "Race and Gender Discrimination in Bargaining for New Cars"). The extant research reveals that Blacks pay higher interest rates on loans, and that, in the case of the most recent sub-prime mortgage loan debacle, Blacks were more likely to be extended sub-prime mortgages than any other group in America. It is also true that many Blacks pay relatively more for insurance. When one takes into account the cost of transportation to and from commercial enterprises, because Blacks normally live further away from the highest quality shopping malls, one must conclude that, while they may pays the same sales price for the items purchased, when one tacks on the transportation cost, Blacks pay more for the same goods. Black Americans must wake up to the fact that they are being shafted all the way around in America. They earn less wages than Whites for the same or similar work, and they must pay more for essentially the same goods than their White counterparts. What is so warm, cozy, and favorable about this outcome? Blacks must recognize that they can do better than this on their own—in their own nation!

We recognize the argument that the United States has used Black labor and ingenuity to produce an enormous capital stock; a level of infrastructure unknown to any other nation in the world. It would be a gargantuan task to reproduce the same level of infrastructure in a Black nation—to the extent that such a nation would be constituted outside of the United States. Black Americans should recognize, however, that a great deal of that infrastructure is duplicative and outmoded—not fit for a world based on material and energy efficiency. Moreover, Black Americans must recognize that materialism is not the key solution to life as originally intended. Economists say that "more is better," but that is not a tautology. Remember the South African Bushmen.

Given the intellect of the African mind, Black Americans must begin to devote time and energy to planning their new nation: Where it should be constituted, the correct governmental structure, and the proper economic structure with particular attention to identifying the proper incentive structure and valuation mechanisms. If Black Americans seeks to plan their new nation on the concept of returning to a world as originally intended, then there must be an emphasis on reuniting with nature—God's creation—in order to create an eternally sustainable environment. Black Americans need to research early civilizations and identify the keys to their longevity, effectiveness, and success. Most importantly, these civilizations' demises should be understood so that similar scenarios are not permitted to unfold. Having said all of that, the bottom line is that the society must be built from the basic building block of a holy Black family that embodies love and communication—a situation that facilitates identifying solutions to problems because everyone has a voice with which to contribute their genius. Understanding all of this should enable Black Americans to realize that they have more to gain by quitting America than by remaining a part of America.

America will fall from her lofty heights, with or without Obama. A Russian social scientist predicted as much in the early 1990s. His prediction has resurfaced of

late (see the story about Igor Panarin's prediction that the U.S. will breakup after the financial and economic crises at http://www.bloomberg.com/apps/news?pid= 20601103&sid=a3sayDZz.QKc&refer=us).
In fact the seeds of a U.S. breakup have already been planted; viz. efforts in Texas to enhance the state's independence (see http://governor.state.tx.us/news/press- release/12227/). If one considers the economic and political circumstances confronting the United States today, then it is not difficult to draw a straight line from a starting point idea of an American breakup to the formation of a Black nation.

This is not to argue that Obama has not had or will not have any effect on the Black American condition. "Black Unemployment and Infotainment," an article that appears in the January 2009 issue of the *Journal of Economic Inquiry* (visit http://papers.ssrn.com/sol3/papers.cfm?abs tract_id=1331693 for the full text of the article) tells the story of Black unemployment being twice that of Whites over the years 1972 to 2002. What we find since the beginning of 2007, however, is a reduction in the ratio of Black to White unemployment. The value has fallen below 2 for several months since the beginning of

2007. The point being that with the onset of the Obama campaign and media coverage of an impressive Black mind, hiring officials may have begun to alter their hiring decisions, and may have begun to hire more Blacks relative to White candidates. It may be that they surmised that Blacks were not all comedians, singers, dancers, and athletes, but that they, too, had intellects sufficient to contribute positively to the bottom lines of firms. Alternatively, it could be that Blacks have positioned themselves in industries that are more recession proof.[6]

We can see an Obama effect elsewhere. Some ingenious social scientists used the Obama election to test the "stereotype threat" hypothesis. The hypothesis is that stereotypes are self-fulfilling. For example, it is widely believed that men are more mathematically inclined than women. Consequently, if prior to a mathematics examination this idea of male-to-female superiority in mathematics is presented to test takers, the examination scores will reflect the expected outcome: Male test takers will perform more excellently on the

---

[6] For more on this topic see "Black Unemployment: An Obama Effect";
http://www.BlackEconomics.org/BE&Lit/BUAOE.pdf).

examination than they normally would, while females will perform more poorly than they normally would. In connection with the recent research, the social scientists tested general performance on an examination with a wide range of Graduate Record Examination (GRE) questions. History has produced a profile of White versus Black performance on the GRE, with the distribution of White scores on the examination being statistically different and with a higher average score than Black scores. In this case, the examination was given to a group of Black and White test-takers across a wide age range before and after the 2008 presidential election. The researchers found that Black and White test-takers who took the examination before the election performed in a way that was consistent with the traditional gap in Black and White GRE scores. However, after the election, researchers found that the traditional gap was reduced considerably. Apparently, the stereotype threat was ameliorated somewhat by the Obama election. As the Obama campaign mantra goes, "Yes We Can" must have sunk into the psyche of White and Black Americans to the point of having an effect on GRE performance. (See Sam Dillon's, "Study Sees Obama Effect as Lifting Black Test-

Takers" at http://www.nytimes.com/2009/01/23/educati on/23gap.html?_r=1&scp=1&sq=obama%2 0test%20scores&st=cse.)

What other effects will Obama have? We were impressed by the multiplicity of Black youth who voiced somewhat unexpected life expectations shortly before and after the November 2008 election. Whereas it was expected that little Black boys would aspire to be football or basketball players or rappers, it was surprising and refreshing to hear so many say that they wanted to achieve other life goals when invited to do so by the media leading up to and after the election. Our recollection is that a few even said that they wanted to be president. Why not president of a Black American nation?

This raises the question, "To which fields should Black Americans aspire?" The current reality is that Black Americans have self-selected to concentrate in eight occupations. Table 1 shows that nearly 60% of Black employed persons work in these eight occupations. The point is not to argue against Blacks working in these occupations. There must be some type of optimization behavior going on here. Unfortunately, enough research has not been undertaken to identify what is being optimized. However, given the benefits that generally accrue to outstanding Black performers in other fields, namely science and technology, one must enquire about the low representation of Blacks in those fields. We must not overlook that some Blacks perform scientific and technology work as part of their roles in *Educational services*, *Healthcare services, except hospitals*, and *Hospitals* occupations.

Table 1.—Top Black American Occupations, 2007

| Line No. | Occupational Title | Employment Shares | Cumulative Percentage |
|---|---|---|---|
| 1. | Retail trade | 10.7% | 10.7% |
| 2. | Educational services | 8.6% | 19.3% |
| 3. | Healthcare services, except hospitals | 8.6% | 27.9% |
| 4. | Transportation and warehousing | 7.5% | 35.4% |
| 5. | Public administration | 6.7% | 42.1% |
| 6. | Hospitals | 5.9% | 48.0% |
| 7. | Food service and drinking places | 5.4% | 53.4% |
| 8. | Administration and support services | 5.3% | 58.7% |

Source: U.S. Department of Labor, Bureau of Labor Statistics, "Employed persons by race, Hispanic origin, and industry, 2007 annual averages"

What must Blacks do about these occupational concentrations? If Blacks are to begin to plan for the formation of a Black American nation, then they must begin to ensure that there is Black expertise in fields critical to nation formation: Economics, Public Administration, Engineering, Science, Health, Education, etc. Because such occupational diversity does not exist today in Black America on a deep enough level, a strategy must be developed to create it. This can be accomplished in the same way that Black Americans have achieved every other important goal. Black Americans must identify, at early ages, youth who have the capability of fulfilling key roles, then motivate and stimulate those youth to pursue the correct courses of actions that will result in their appropriate training and preparation to assume such roles in a Black nation. Black Americans are a 40-million-strong nation within the American nation, and that population will constitute a sizeable separate nation. There will be a need for large operations to meet the physical needs of the nation. It is critical that Black Americans begin now to ensure that sufficient numbers of Black Americans are trained to fulfill critical occupational requirements.

As a credit to Booker T. Washington's efforts, once upon a time, there were a sizeable number of Black carpenters, electricians, plumbers, auto mechanics, etc. Today, one would be hard-pressed to identify in the yellow pages of any city or town in America many qualified Black carpenters, electricians, plumbers, or auto mechanics. Research needs to be performed to determine why there has been a disappearance of these skilled craftsmen, and to determine how to reverse the current outcome. If you cannot build a house, how can you house a family? If you cannot house a family, how can you form a nation? If you cannot build or repair transportation equipment, how can you travel to your new homeland?

What about Black Americans' physical well-being? The Middle-Passage was a perfect mechanism for selecting the strongest physical specimens for slavery. If one survived the Middle-Passage, then one was likely to have a very hearty and healthy constitution. The American experiment, however, due to the sheer stress that Black Americans face each day, has produced a people that become sick too often and die too young. Black American lifestyle choices also contribute greatly to illness and to early death. The Honorable Elijah Muhammad, the Black Jesus, wrote *How to Eat to Live (see* http://www.seventhfam.com/temple/books/e attolive_one/eat1index.htm), which provided great guidance on diet for Black Americans. How many Black Americans know about that book and follow its dietary principles? Too few.

What is killing Black America most? The following are the top "Relative Age-Adjusted Incidence of Death per 100,000 Population for Blacks Relative to Whites by Disease (in percent) for the year 2002":[7]

- Heart Disease (30.3%)
- Cancer (24.6%)
- Stroke (40.8%)
- Diabetes (214.3%)
- Unintentional Injuries (0.98%)
- Homicides (567.5%)
- Nephritis (Inflammation of the kidney) (statistics not available)

---

[7] The sources of these data are: http://www.cdc.gov/omhd/Populations/BAA/BAA.htm ; and http://www.cdc.gov/nchs/data/hus/hus04trend.pdf#0 3. Both sources were retrieved from the Internet on September 15, 2007

- Chronic Lower Respiratory Disease (0.69%)
- HIV AIDS (865.3%)
- Septicemia (Bacteria in the Blood) (statistics not available)

These data may be interpreted to mean, for example, that on an age-adjusted basis, Black Americans have a 567.5% greater probability of dying of homicide than White Americans. What's up with that? Is America such a great place to live if one's chances of being killed are 567.5% greater than one's White counterpart?

Black American lifestyle choices—i.e., what they eat, drink, and do—are causing them to die in ways and at rates not experienced by the White population. When you add stress to the equation, you add fuel to the fire of death. Scientists are already showing that stress is a critical contributor to the incidence of diseases such as cancer, particularly in Black women. Black women have the hardest job in America. Not only must they work and prove themselves every day in a racist and discriminating world, but they must also play the roles of mom and pop in a family that quite often has no father. In too many cases, Black women have no one to share the burden of family problem solving. They work and worry. They worry and work. The pressure and stress are unbearable. Their bodies break down and cancer leaps in and kills them. Black man, you cry to God, "Why did you let them (the White world) beat us, rape our women, and murder our sons?" Should you not ask yourself, "How and why do I let the vagaries of life destroy and kill my Black queen—my sweetness, my honey?"

Some argue that if Blacks were more educated, then circumstances would improve. What is the story on Black education? For 2007, of the Black population that was 18 years or older (21.6 million), about 20% had not graduated from high school, about 36% had completed high school, about 20% had some college, about 8% had associate (two-year) degrees, about 12% had a bachelor's degree, about 4% had a master's degree, about 0.7% held professional degrees, and about 0.5% held doctoral degrees. If we were to think about Dubois' talented 10th, then we have surpassed his expectations because well over 10% of the Black population has a bachelor's degree or more. It seems problematic, however, that in the 21st century a fifth (20%) of the Black population is without a high school diploma. Nevertheless, if we ignore the quality of education issue, the educational profile of Black America supersedes that of many nations. Black America has more than sufficient brain power to form its own nation. (These data are available from the U.S. Census Bureau; http://www.census.gov/population/www/soc demo/education/cps2006.html.)

On the other hand, if Black Americans are to excel at nation building, then a simple, yet very important transformation is required when it comes to education. As discussed above, there is a need to devote more energy to science and technology. This can be most easily accomplished by reducing the time and energy devoted to athletics. Many Black Americans argue that Black youth devote too much time to athletics and that they do so irrationally. We argue that this behavior is not irrational. The fact of the matter is that every Black child knows someone who knows someone who has, at a minimum, obtained a college athletic scholarship, which is the gateway to professional sports—the big contract, the millions, the bling-bling. Therefore, it is not irrational for these youth to pursue athletic goals.

What Black America needs is an educational program that fully informs Black youth and their parents on the facts about athletics. They need to know the true probabilities of reaching the professional ranks and the likelihood of capturing the high valued contracts. Relatedly, they need to know the role of agents and taxes when it comes to those contracts and to be told exactly what percentage of the "big dollars" the athletes actually secure for themselves. They need to know the simple facts about the extent to which contracts are based on incentives and that the "contract amount" is usually not completely guaranteed. They need to learn about the physical cost of being an athlete—including the shortened lifespan and/or the debilitated quality of life that results from the wear and tear on the body from professional competition. They need to know about the life of a college athlete—the pressure to perform to the exclusion, if necessary, of the actual learning process in college. They need to know the statistics concerning how many collegiate athletes actually graduate from college. They need to know that athletics is not the best game in town. On the flip side, they need to know the wealth that can await them from super-star-like performance in the science and technology fields, and the joy obtainable from developing a new product, method, or technology that can change lives and transform societies and the world. This is no slight on hearing the crowd cheer. We must remember that the cheer in an arena lasts for seconds—a few minutes at most. On the other hand, the love and respect that is engendered by scientists or engineers who solve critical problems that save lives, communities, and even nations lasts a lifetime and beyond.

Let us move toward a conclusion by referring again to the lecture by the late Dr. John Henrick Clarke entitled "The African Mind." In it he points out that (and we paraphrase) "State formation is like running a candy store. If one cannot run a candy store, then one cannot run a state." In other words, operating a state is about ensuring that the people remain busy meeting their physical, psychological, and spiritual needs. Put another way, state formation and operation is inextricably linked to commerce—business. All people of the world are inclined to do business. Some are more preoccupied with this challenge than others. Africans had, and have, a great commercial tradition. When one thinks of a typical or traditional market, the mind goes immediately to farmers markets, which take us back to the African market place. Therefore, Black Americans have always been skilled at doing business and they have flourished in developing business where they have not been prevented from doing so. Even today, we are occasionally amazed to hear about a young Black mind that has master minded a major drug ring. The press writes, "He was an expert businessman." We recall the great independent commercial centers that Blacks built in early 20th century America, such as in Tulsa, Oklahoma or Rosewood, Florida, which were ultimately destroyed in 1921 and 1923, respectively, by those envious of that success. What we learn about the first census of Black and Women owned business in the United States, which was conducted in 1969, is that there were over 300 thousand Black-owned businesses. What is somewhat surprising is that 28% of those Black-owned businesses were large enough to support employees. But then desegregation and integration proceeded to disrupt the economic base of Black America. If we role the clock forward about 30 years to 2002 (the latest year for which data are available), we find that the percentage of Black-owned businesses with employees has shrunk to about 8%. (These data are available from the U.S. Department of Commerce, Bureau of the Census, Quinquennial *Censuses of Women and Minority-Owned Businesses*.) This is an explicit and factual tale about how desegregation and integration harmed Black America. Yes, there are significantly more Black businesses today (more than one million in 2002) than in 1969; and naturally so, because the Black population has grown. However, the percentage of businesses that are large enough to support employees has fallen off tremendously. Herein lies another reason why the Black unemployment rate has traditionally been so high. Why should Black Americans expect others to be their major source of employment? Employ yourself. Form successful Black businesses that can employ Black workers. That's what state formation will require.

We have highlighted numerous problems faced by Blacks in America. The new mantra is "put it behind you, get over it, slavery ended over 150 years ago." Given the evidence presented herein, it must be difficult for Black Americans to "put it behind them, and get over it." These conditions described in this chapter are not associated with the 17th, 18th, 19th, or even 20th centuries. These are conditions today in this new 21$^{st}$ century. One can pose the rhetorical question, "Are things getting better or worse." However, the answer is crystal clear. For Black Americans, some may prosper, but many continue to suffer the scourge of poverty, income inequality, discrimination, racism, sickness, disease, and a life without real hope that conditions will improve tomorrow.

At the end of 2008, the picture turned bleaker for many Black Americans as the global financial and economic crisis came into full view. The National Bureau of Economic Research says that the U.S. recession began in December of 2007. Nevertheless, unemployment began to rise rapidly in 2008. Loans dried up, especially for Blacks. As a matter of fact, the finger pointing about the sub-prime mortgage crisis became very vicious toward Black Americans. The evidence is that the preponderance of NINJA sub-prime loans did not go to Black Americans (NINJA is for "no income , no job, and no assets"). One should expect as much. In the past, the saying was that Blacks were "the last hired and the first fired" during a recession. Now it seems reasonable to add that, when a recession occurs, blame Black Americans.

The current financial economic and global crisis, whether orchestrated or concocted, is causing misery around the world for many working class and poor people. What we should not forget is that the wealthy own and control so much of the wealth that they do not stand to suffer greatly—in the main. If one is wealthy—in the top 10% of the income distribution—then it is likely that one is trained in business or economics, and/or that one has a financial adviser. If you are wealthy and were ignorant enough to select a financial adviser who did not prevent you from losing considerable sums during the economic downturn, then shame on you. Maybe you don't deserve to play with the big boys. However, for many poor and working class Americans and people around the world, their only savings were tied up in retirement funds that were invested in securities the value of which evaporated rapidly. In many cases, the working poor may not have known what to do to prevent their investments from evaporating. What they know today is that they may have to revise their retirement plans considerably. The problem is that today's financial markets do not offer many opportunities that provide good prospects for growth and that embody minimal risk.

It is in this context that President Barack Obama enters the scene. The world is looking upon the United States as the major cause of the crisis. The world is looking at the United States as the key to a recovery. (Notably, China is also viewed as a possible economic savior.) Not only is President Obama faced with a financial and economic crisis of historical proportions, he has two wars to resolve, the problem of major entitlement programs with growing unfunded liabilities, an educational system that is producing substandard students when compared with the rest of the world, and a healthcare system that continues to inhale an increasing share of the nation's gross domestic product. And those are just the top four or five concerns. It would take a genius and magician of universal proportions to tackle all of these problems at once. In comes the "Magic Negro."[8]

The European mind in America fully understands where we are in history. They

---

[8] If a myth exists ("Magic Negro"), then it must be backed by some reality. Therefore, we must think that in the course of history, there were Black men who spoke and acted with the power of God. Men who said "Be" and "it was." President Obama does not have that power.

understand that their 6000 year reign has ended. They understand that it is time for the reign of Christ. Who is the Christ? In Part I, we asserted that the Honorable Elijah Muhammad was Jesus the Christ. Therefore, his followers are those that can represent the Christ—the Black man and woman of America. Knowing this, the European mind has inserted a seemingly Black-American into a seat of power, hoping to engender favor from the Lord of the Worlds. At least they hope to use this trick to cloud the picture long enough so as to disrupt the course of history and to retain their grasp on power. How will the European mind attempt to disrupt the course of history? By manufacturing a representative of Black America and by discrediting that representative so that when Black America awakens and attempts to seize its rightful leadership seat, the world will not recognize that leadership. In other words, the plan of the European is to discredit Barack Obama and to create the appearance of an inept and incapable leader. Consider the pace at which Obama's "helpers" have assisted him in obtaining nearly three trillion dollars for purposes of resolving the financial and economic crisis. Also consider the rate at which those funds have disappeared into thin air with little measurable result. Ask yourself whether the fox is in the hen house. Ask yourself whether there is a Wall Street-to-Washington revolving door. Ask yourself whether that revolving door can only be entered and exited by those who rule Wall Street and the U.S. Treasury on Pennsylvania Avenue in Washington. Ask yourself why the head of the U.S. central bank (Chairman of the Federal Reserve Board) always (at least for recent decades) has to be Jewish—think Volker, Greenspan, and now Bernanke?

Just as we were enabled to discern that Obama was a shoe-in for the presidency, we can now inform you that the Obama presidency will be a one-term affair. We can assure you that the global economic and financial crisis is not likely to have been fully resolved by 2012. Moreover, the nation's deficit and debt will grow by historical proportions during the Obama Presidency. Obama will be made to appear worse than Herbert Hoover, one of the most despised presidents in the history of the nation because he could not resolve the economic crisis that was the Great Depression. Because the Obama administration will be unable to right the U.S. economy, not only will the nation that elected him be angry with him and with Black Americans, so will the world. The world will come to despise Black Americans. Therefore, when Black Americans awaken to the anger of America and attempt to exit the nation and establish a Black American nation, they will find little help from abroad.

If you think that all of this is inaccurate, you will be able to assess these assertions in a limit of time—by 2012. In fact, you will not have to wait that long. These events will unfold quickly. Recognize that efforts to discredit the Black male have been ongoing for the last 6000 years. Nevertheless, the Black man is still standing. He has been beaten down, but he has not been defeated. Like Abraham, we must ask, "Is there one righteous Black man still in America." If there is, then will God come to his rescue and to the rescue of his people? The answer is that "God's will SHALL be done." The Black Man's Savior has come. He planted the seeds and spoke the words that must come to fruition. Not only will the Black man survive, he will achieve the ends that were prophesied by the Honorable Elijah Muhammad and that are written about in *The Holy Bible* and the *Holy Qur'an*. "If my people, who are called by my name humble themselves, and pray and seek my face, and turn from their wicked ways, then I will hear from heaven, and will forgive their sin and heal their land" (*The Holy Bible, 2$^{nd}$ Chronicles* 7:14).  In other words, Black America has a choice to make.  Assuming that they make the correct choice, then they can rest assured that all will be as it should because, "Man [the White mind] plans, and God plans. God is the Best of Planners" (*Holy Qur'an*, 3:54).

# Part III: Future

<u>Opening</u>

In storefront Pentecostal and Baptist Churches across America, preachers invite their congregations to praise God. They urge them to invoke the spirit of God so that they can all receive a rush of good feeling and a release. Many times, they will command their congregation to exalt: "Jesus is here!" What they do not seem to know is that the second coming of Jesus has already occurred before their very eyes in the person of the Honorable Elijah Muhammad. He was here. Now he is gone. What remains is his teachings and his word, which must be fulfilled. In addition, his followers remain and they must perform the tasks—run the races—that have been set before them.

What does it mean to say that Jesus the Christ lived in our lifetime? What does it matter that Elijah Muhammad was the Black Man's Jesus? It means that the key aspects of the Bible have been fulfilled. What we now know is the mystery of the Bible. What is that mystery? The mystery is that even the black cover of the Bible was, and is, a sign. It means that what is inside the Bible is for the Black man, and mainly for the Black man alone. It spells out his future. It is a future that involves a 430-year sojourn in America—after which the Black man will come out with great substance.

If key aspects of the Bible have been fulfilled, then that means that the remaining portions will be fulfilled. Which Bible prophecies that are most important are to be fulfilled? We can expect that followers of Christ shall enter heaven. What is that heaven? Heaven will be a place where the Black man and woman shall never die; i.e., they shall practice their religion perfectly and transmit their living souls from their dying bodies into the living bodies of their children. It will also be a place of peace relative to the hell that Black Americans have suffered in the Wilderness of North America. There will be no sickness, no pain, and no sorrow. Why? Suffering will disappear because Black Americans will not experience the anguish and turmoil that they had to endure in America. We cannot contend that the streets will be paved with gold if one is concerned about physical gold. However, if one is concerned about the golden aspects of life (i.e., good families, good friends, and food, clothing, and shelter), then all of these golden aspects of life will pave the course of Black life in the new nation.

*The Holy Bible* says, "First seek ye the kingdom of God and his righteousness and all of these things will be added unto you" (*The Holy Bible*, St. Matthew 6:33). What is the Kingdom of God? It is the place where God reigns. If Jesus and God are one, and if the Honorable Elijah Muhammad is Jesus, then his knowledge shall reign in the new Black nation because his followers will use his knowledge (gained from God—Fard Muhammad) to create and operate the nation. Once the Black man seeks, finds, and builds the Kingdom of God using the righteous principles that were provided by the Honorable Elijah Muhammad, then all of these things will be added. What things? The things that will be added will be those things that the Black man and woman have so earnestly desired. A good home, a good family, good relations in their community, and peace.

As indicated in Part I on the "Past," we entertained the question of the location of this new Black nation. Some Black

Americans believe that it should be within the Continental United States—probably in the south. Others might agree with our assertion that it is to be in Canada, which becomes Canaan by removing a "d" and adding an "n." At the end (d – n) of Black Americans' sojourn, they are likely to find themselves somewhere in the Americas. How are they to up and get a piece of land for 40-plus million people? If you have a "dead" mentality, you might consider plotting ways to take the land. However, we were reminded by a teacher that it is better to ask than to steal. The White man has always accused the Black man of stealing. Now we know that proclivity reflects the psychological phenomenon known as transference. The biggest thief in the history of the world would lynch a Black man for taking food to feed his family after the boss cheated him out of the wages due him. We know this to be true. Therefore, Black America should avoid even the appearance of evil. Consequently, Black Americans should identify the current owners of the land that God has promised and begin to negotiate to gain access to the land. They should offer to purchase the land; but it is very likely that the rightful owners of the land will gift the land to them. Who are these rightful owners likely to be?

They are likely to be Native Americans. History is clear about the theft of American land by Europeans. Black Americans should make every effort to avoid committing the same evil that the White man committed when it comes to our Asiatic Brothers, the Native Americans. Many Black Americans have considerable Native American blood, and so, to a great extent, have every right to request land from their blood relatives. But in case our Native American brothers decide that they would like to be compensated for the land, then Black Americans should be prepared to pay.

As part of the negotiations for the transfer of the land, Black Americans should provide a plan of sustainable development. Native Americans and Black people of the world have a history of living according to the laws of nature—God's rules. It stands to reason that Native Americans would be quite pleased to know that the land that they transfer to Black Americans will be cared for properly. Moreover, Black Americans should arrange an agreement with Native Americans that involves "sharing the land." Black Americans should be given the right to use the land as agreed; however, Native Americans should be able to share in the land.   Native American people are quite independent, so it is unlikely that they will need to share the land.   Nevertheless, because they were the first to occupy this beautiful America, they should have the opportunity to move around the land and use it as required.

Now that it is clear how land for the new Black nation is to be acquired, let us discuss key aspects of development of the new Black nation.   Let's consider seven aspects of development that must take place: Religion, government, family, health, education, commerce, and history. Because the new Black nation will be God's kingdom, it is expected that Black Americans will adopt and apply teachings provided by God (Jesus, the Honorable Elijah Muhammad) in order to establish and operate the new nation effectively. Therefore, the thoughts that are provided below are only intended to serve as reflections of those teachings.   The thoughts will be brief.

Religion.--The Black man's God, the one who molded his mind into shape, Fard Muhammad, begot his son, the Black Jesus (the Honorable Elijah Muhammad) and gave him to the Black world in order to become its savior. But there is also "God of all the Worlds." In the Islamic tradition, that God is Allah. Given the source of the Black man's Freedom, Justice, and Equality, it seems clear that he has moved beyond the religion of Christianity, and must formulate his religion around the teachings of his Jesus, his God, and the God Allah. What we have here is a trinity: The Father, the Son, and the Holy Ghost. The Father is Fard Muhammad, the Son is Elijah Muhammad, and the Holy Ghost is God Allah. The two former parts of the trinity have been dealt with extensively. We should take a moment to elaborate on the latter part. The Holy Ghost, the Great Spirit, is that essential aspect of creation—the life spirit and life mind itself. The Holy Ghost is the essential self that is life itself and the guiding force that contains the "DNA" of our lives. It is the energy force that enables us to "live, move, and have our being" (*Holy Bible, Acts of the Apostles* 17:28). It is also the quiet voice that continually urges us to perform the correct behaviors as we transit life. Africans worshipped or respected and honored all aspects of nature because they knew that the Holy Ghost—the Great Spirit—was in them all. Therefore, we should worship, respect, and honor the Great Spirit that is the God Allah force that is operating throughout creation to bring it into fulfillment.

If we follow these principles, then we will remain on the correct path to not only fulfilling the teachings and requirements of the Father and the Son, but also of the Great Spirit—the Holy Ghost. It leads us and guides us in all of the ways of truth and righteousness. We should do these things in order to fulfill the Grand Plan of the Great God Allah, the Holy Ghost. What is that plan? God Allah gives us clues about that plan. What we know is that we continuously see that some things materialize in our physical creation out of nothing. What we know is that it seems that the unseen is more powerful and infinite than the seen or finite. Therefore, we may surmise, using *The Holy Bible* as a point of reference, that God created the entire world out of nothing. In the beginning there was only God Allah, his thoughts (the divine and infinite mind) and his power. From that state, the universe began to unfold. Now we have a vast and seemingly infinite physical universe. But what we know about creation is that, that which exists ceases to exist. It fades away. Therefore, it must be true that, one day, the physical universe will cease to exist and return to its former state—it will return to being all wrapped up in God—his divine and infinite mind, and his power. As human beings on planet Earth, our task is to continue our existence until the Great Day when all that has been rolled out will be rolled up. We can all be here for that event because we can perfect our religion (reliving) by, at the points of physical death, inserting our living souls from our dead bodies into the living bodies of our children, grandchildren, and great grand children.

Let's be clear, whatever and however Black Americans formulate their religion in this new nation, it seems logical that that religion will embody these basic concepts and principles.

<u>Government</u>.--Government is designed to provide a framework for living the physical life. The Honorable Elijah Muhammad instructed the Black man to seek Freedom, Justice, and Equality from the American government. It seems reasonable that the Government of the new Black nation would embody these three principles. Whether the new Black nation adopts favorable aspects of Western governmental systems or goes back to the original authors of these

concepts—the people of Africa—the nation should ensure that government facilitate freedom, justice, and equality. Government should ensure every man and woman the right to worship, produce, and contribute to the peaceful formation and evolution of society. As a check on when the new Black nation has modulated its government to perfection, it will be when there will be no need for jails. Notably, if the government of the new Black nation handles domestic affairs effectively, then international affairs will take care of themselves.

Family.--Family is the basic building block of society. Therefore, the new Black nation must ensure that this building block is vibrant and strong. In Part I on the "Past," we made mention of a family that is full of love, respect, and communications such that each member of the family has a voice to contribute his or her genius to the task of family problem solving. The family unit should be complete in and of itself. Therefore, it is hoped that families in the new Black nation will provide for the full spectrum of life, which involves everyone from the new born baby to the 100-plus year-old grandparents or great grandparents. The new Black nation family should return to the African tradition of benefiting from the wisdom of the elders by keeping them in the family—not tossing them away into institutions where there is no love or hope of life. Moreover, how can one perfect the religion (reliving) when one is not near the one in which to continue living at the point of death?

<u>Health</u>.--Health should be a key point of concern in the new Black nation. If the people are not healthy, then they cannot work properly. If they cannot work properly, then the nation cannot be constructed properly. If the nation is not constructed properly, then it will crumble and fall. The top-of-the-pyramid issue when it comes to Black health is mental health. The nearly 400-year experience in America has not boded well for Black self-esteem and mental health. Therefore, it is critical that great efforts be made in the new Black nation to ensure the proper mental health. Sound mental health is characterized by a people who truly love themselves, and then assume the individual and collective responsibility of safeguarding their physical health. "Where the head goes, the body is bound to follow."

The new Black nation should take heed to an important warning. The new Black nation must pay careful attention to the role of viruses. Those who may seek to destroy the new Black nation may attempt to do so through the use of viruses.

Education.--Education is a continuous process of tilling the mind so that it can use the body to produce the requirements of life. We have already discussed the education and the mis-education of Black Americans in Part II on "Present." The new Black nation must develop an educational system that has the capacity to prepare the population to produce the goods and services that it needs in the present period as well as for future periods. If one is learning how to produce for today, then one is already behind the curve. It is critical that education in the new Black nation emphasize the future so that the nation is not surprised by unfolding developments. A worse-case scenario is for the nation to be unable to meet unexpected requirements, especially when those requirements would have been easily discernible had sufficient attention been given to the future.

Commerce.--Commerce of the nation is like "running a candy store." You'll recall these words from the great Black historian, the late Dr. John Henrick Clarke. The essential points to comprehend here is that all efforts should be made to avoid the development of corruption in the commercial system of the new Black nation. If the government is to be based on freedom, justice, and equality, then that should be the mantra for the commercial system as well. Entrepreneurs, workers, and consumers should be viewed equally—all contributing to the well-being of the new Black nation. Entrepreneurs should not be valued more highly than workers or consumers for their role in the nation's economy. There should be complete freedom to engage justly in commerce and to purchase the products and services that are required. We caution the nation concerning the formation of greed. What should be taught and what should be valued are citizens who exert full energy each day to perform their tasks— whatever they might be—in service to the nation. If these principles are taught, and if opportunities are sufficiently open, then there will be no "incentive" issues in the new nation's economy. It will turn out that there is a place for everyone and for everyone a place. In order to ensure this outcome, transparent information must flow freely so that fully informed and rational decisions can be taken.

<u>History</u>.--History is a record.  But the new Black nation must be wise about history. Just as in the case of *The Holy Bible* and the *Holy Qur'an*, where wise men wrote history in advance, men and women of the new Black nation must gather periodically to write their history in advance.  These wise Black persons should achieve a heightened state of consciousness in order to "see down the road a piece" and hear and sense the mood, sentiments, and actions of the people in the far off distance. Given that insight, they can prepare an accurate history, which will provide clear guidance for the nation to follow.  In the Western world, it is called planning.  Wise Black people recognize it for what it is— writing one's history.

<u>Conclusion</u>

The Black or African mind is the original mind.  It thinks more like God than any other mind.  The Great God Allah—the Great Spirit, the Holy Ghost—formed the Black mind (man) out of the dust of the earth.  Earth, generally, is dark or black in color, that is how we know that the Black man is the original man.  Of course, we also have Dr. Leakey's findings as evidence. We know that we were part of the formation of the earliest civilizations. If we were here first and if we are still here, then that means that we were part of it all. When we take the time to go back and study the early civilizations, we can learn the secrets about life and this world—including the secret of eternal life. How does one live forever? If one is focused on the physical body living forever, then one will miss the boat every time. One must move beyond the physical to the metaphysical, to the everlasting. What is everlasting? The soul is everlasting. What is the soul? The soul is that part of you that makes you who you are. It is the life force in you that has wings and that is looking out of your body through your two eyes. It is anxious to get out of your body, to flit hither and thither, and to do all of the things that your mind thinks about. It is like quick silver. It can travel across the room, across the neighborhood, across the city, state, country, around the world, and throughout the universe if it was free to roam. A disembodied soul wanders and communicates with other disembodied souls. It even communicates with souls in physical bodies that are keen enough to hear, feel, and touch it. We comprehend these things about living souls. At the same time, we value the physical life that God enables us to experience. The constraint on physical life is that the body deteriorates and ultimately dies—it returns to dust. However, God placed us in the Garden of Eden called Earth so that we could enjoy the physical life forever. The problem is that some of us lost touch with the knowledge of how to live forever.

The *Holy Qur'an (3:102)* admonishes us to "die not except in a state of Islam." In other words, be certain that when you die, you are clean, pure, and ready to submit to the will of God. If one submits to God's will and allows the body to die at the appropriate time, then one's soul can exit the dying body and immediately enter the living body of one prepared to receive one's soul. Which body should that be? Just as we pass books, clothes, and wealth down through a family, we can also pass souls down through the family. How often have you seen and heard someone say, "Son or daughter, you didn't used to, but now you are looking more and more like your father or mother." Of course the father and mother have already deceased, but they have continued their lives in their sons and daughters. The bodies of the sons and daughters have taken on the appearance of the fathers and mothers because the fathers' and mothers' souls brought their likenesses with them when they entered the sons and daughters. In other words, this practice of eternal life has been with us. It's just that among Black Americans, our troubled concerns with this life made it difficult for us to focus on the important things in life and to practice our religion (reliving). Now the truth has come, and the truth has set us free. Free from what. Free from the death, because now we know how to live forever.

Given the new knowledge that God has brought back to our remembrance, we can undertake the gargantuan task of building a new Black nation. We are God's chosen people who shall build a heavenly nation on earth. It will not be easy. It will take more than a generation. Yet we will live through it all, because we now know how to live forever. We will help build the nation during this life. When our physical bodies die, we will live again in the bodies of our children, grandchildren, and great grandchildren, and continue to build the nation until it is completed. No dying over there, no pain, and no sorrow. Just joy and peace. Aren't you happy to know that you are going to build a new nation like that?

If Black Americans do not choose to build their new nation, then the outcome will be quite disparaging. What would be the outcome? It is painful to imagine that a Great People—actually, the strongest of a great people—would endure the Middle Passage and over 400 years as strangers in a strange land only to disappear—cease to exist. If Black Americans do not escape America, the current course of events will continue. In the end, it is likely that those Black Americans who fail to conform and sublimate themselves perfectly to the Western mind will be destroyed. Those who conform and sublimate themselves perfectly will find that they are completely absorbed into a Western mind. It could be that four or five generations hence, the Black American that we know today would no longer exist. His skin color would have changed and the texture of his hair would have changed—his physical nature would no longer be discernible. Most importantly, his mind—his will to control his destiny--will have changed. He would become a zombie-like creature like the remainder of the Western world—a people without a true and righteous purpose because their goals and purposes are wrapped in materialism, the finite. Black Americans who hate their Black self and love White skin and straight hair might be proud to disappear among the dead. However, every Black man, woman, and child who seek a better future, a better place, and a better life—i.e., eternal life— must reject this choice.

May the Peace, Mercy, and Blessings of God the Father (Fard Muhammad) and his Son (the Honorable Elijah Muhammad—the Black Jesus Christ) be upon you, and may you have the fellowship of the Holy Ghost— the Great God Allah, the Great Spirit— forever.

May 1, 390